Published by Ethan Starke
5640 Santa Monica Blvd
Los Angeles, California, 90038

ISBN: 979-8-9922475-3-4
First Edition

This book is intended as a practical resource and informational guide. It is not a substitute for professional counseling or therapy. The author and publisher assume no liability for outcomes related to the use of this book.

Curate a Date:
The Companion Guide
Exercises, Tools, and Resources for Meaningful Connections

Bringing Love to Life –

A Companion to *Curate a Date*

Love isn't just about grand gestures or perfect moments; it's about the everyday efforts, shared experiences, and small surprises that keep relationships thriving. When writing *Curate a Date*, we explored the art and science of creating meaningful connections, emphasizing the power of thoughtful dates and shared growth. This companion handbook and journal builds on that foundation, offering practical tools and inspiration to make the journey of love both easier and more rewarding.

While *Curate a Date* focused on ideas and strategies, this handbook turns theory into action. Think of it as your personal toolkit for planning memorable moments, nurturing intimacy, and growing as both an individual and a partner. Whether you're looking to plan an unforgettable date, deepen your connection, or simply reflect on your relationship, this companion is here to guide you—without the stress of overthinking or the pressure of perfection.

What This Handbook Offers

Part 1: Practical Tools for Dating

This section is all about turning ideas into experiences. You'll find customizable tools like the **Date Night Planner**, which helps you design dates tailored to your relationship's unique rhythm. Whether you're aiming for something adventurous, cozy, or creative, the planner will walk you through each step, ensuring you have all the details covered.

We've also included **conversation starters and prompts** to keep the spark alive and foster meaningful dialogue. These aren't your average icebreakers; they're designed to uncover hidden dreams, shared values, and even a little lighthearted fun. From the early days of dating to long-term relationships, these questions will help you connect on a deeper level.

For those moments when you want to show love in the smallest, sweetest ways, the **Simple Romantic Gestures** list is your go-to. Sometimes, it's not about big plans but tiny acts of kindness—a favorite treat left on their desk, a handwritten note, or an impromptu dance in the kitchen. These ideas are quick, thoughtful, and guaranteed to make your partner feel cherished.

Finally, **Activity Templates** provide a structured way to create special moments. Whether it's crafting a scavenger hunt, designing a themed date, or building a bucket list together, these templates offer both inspiration and practicality, ensuring that your time together feels memorable and unique.

Part 2: Resources and Inspiration

This section is for those who want to dig deeper into the "why" behind great relationships. We've included a curated list of **further reading and listening**, featuring books, podcasts, and articles that complement the ideas in this handbook. Organized by themes like emotional intelligence, mindfulness, and modern dating tools, these resources will inspire and empower you to approach love with fresh perspectives.

Understanding the language of relationships is key, so we've added a **Glossary of Terms** to define important concepts like "intentional dating" and "emotional deposits." These definitions will give you the confidence to approach your relationship with clarity and purpose, making even the most abstract ideas feel accessible.

Part 3: Reflection and Journaling

The final section invites you to pause, reflect, and grow. With **Reflection Journal Templates**, you'll have space to explore your own feelings, memories, and hopes. Prompts like "What did I admire most about my partner today?" or "How has our relationship grown this month?" encourage both introspection and celebration.

For couples, the **Relationship Check-In** provides a structured way to discuss strengths, challenges, and goals. By setting aside time to assess your journey together, you can ensure that your relationship remains dynamic and intentional.

Finally, **Celebrating Milestones** helps you document the moments that matter most. Whether it's a memorable anniversary, a first trip together, or simply a perfect evening at home, this space lets you capture your shared story in a way that feels personal and meaningful.

Why This Handbook Matters

Relationships, like anything worth pursuing, require effort—but that doesn't mean they should feel like work. This handbook is designed to make love feel lighthearted, engaging, and endlessly rewarding. By combining practical tools with moments of reflection, it ensures that your relationship remains a source of joy, inspiration, and growth.

More than a guide, this handbook is an invitation. It invites you to see dating as an adventure, to approach love with curiosity and creativity, and to celebrate the small, everyday moments that make life together so extraordinary. Whether you're planning your next date or reflecting on your relationship's journey, let this book be your companion in curating a love story that feels uniquely and beautifully yours.

Part 1: Practical Tools for Dating

Date Night Planner

Planning a date can feel daunting, especially when life gets busy. The Date Night Planner is designed to take the guesswork out of organizing memorable experiences. Whether you're aiming for a romantic evening, a fun adventure, or a quiet night in, this tool will guide you step-by-step to ensure your time together feels thoughtful and special.

How to Use This Planner

1. Set the Mood: Decide on the type of date you want (e.g., adventurous, relaxing, creative). Think about your partner's preferences and your shared interests.
2. Plan the Details: Use the prompts below to map out the time, location, activities, and any special touches.
3. Add a Personal Touch: Incorporate something unique to your relationship, like a favorite song, inside joke, or shared memory.
4. Reflect: After the date, take a moment to write down how it went and what you both enjoyed most.

Prompts for Planning

- What type of date are we planning (e.g., casual, romantic, adventurous)?
- Where will the date take place? (Consider places meaningful to your relationship.)
- What activities will we include?
- How can I personalize the experience? (E.g., adding a favorite treat, revisiting a shared memory.)
- Do we need to prepare or bring anything special?

Your Date Night Plan

Your Date Night Plan

Conversation Starters and Prompts

Great conversations are the heartbeat of any relationship. They help us uncover dreams, share laughter, and deepen our understanding of one another. This section offers a curated list of conversation prompts designed to suit every stage of a relationship. Whether it's your first date or your fiftieth, these questions are sure to spark meaningful dialogue and bring you closer together.

How to Use This Section

- Choose a few prompts before your date or let the conversation flow naturally by keeping this list handy.
- Mix lighthearted questions with deeper ones to create balance.
- Be an active listener—focus on your partner's answers and ask follow-ups to show genuine interest.

Prompts for Every Occasion

1. Getting to Know Each Other

    What's your favorite childhood memory?

    If you could live anywhere in the world, where would it be and why?

    What's something you've always wanted to try but haven't yet?

2. Deepening Emotional Connection

    What's one fear or challenge you've overcome that you're proud of?

What's a lesson you've learned that has shaped who you are today?

What does love mean to you?

3. Lighthearted and Fun

If you could time travel, would you visit the past or the future?

What's the strangest food you've ever tried?

If you were a superhero, what would your superpower be?

4. Exploring Shared Values

What's one thing you're most passionate about?

How do you define success?

What's one tradition you'd love to start or maintain in a relationship?

5. Building Future Dreams

What's one place you'd love to visit together?

If we had unlimited time and resources, what's the first thing we'd do?

How do you imagine spending a perfect weekend five years from now?

Our Favorite Questions

 "A great relationship is about two things: appreciating the similarities and respecting the differences."
— Unknown

Our Favorite Questions

Simple Romantic Gestures

Love doesn't always require elaborate plans or expensive gifts. Sometimes, the simplest gestures leave the most lasting impressions. This section is dedicated to small, thoughtful actions that can brighten your partner's day and remind them how much they mean to you. These ideas are easy to incorporate into daily life, ensuring your relationship stays vibrant and full of warmth.

How to Use This Section

- Choose a gesture that resonates with your partner's preferences or love language.
- Don't overthink it—spontaneity often makes the gesture even more meaningful.
- Use this list as inspiration and personalize it to reflect your unique relationship.

Everyday Romantic Gestures

1. Words of Affirmation

   Leave a sticky note on their mirror with a compliment or a simple "I love you."

   Write them a heartfelt letter and tuck it into their bag or pocket.

   Text them something sweet and unexpected during the day.

2. Acts of Service

> Prepare their favorite breakfast or coffee in the morning.
>
> Handle a chore they dislike without being asked.
>
> Warm up their car or pack them a snack for the day ahead.

3. Quality Time

> Plan a surprise evening with no distractions—just the two of you.
>
> Take a walk together at sunset, leaving phones behind.
>
> Start a new tradition, like Sunday morning pancakes or Friday movie nights.

4. Gift Giving

> Pick up their favorite treat on your way home.
>
> Create a playlist of songs that remind you of them.
>
> Surprise them with a small token related to an inside joke or shared memory.

5. Physical Touch

> Hold their hand during a quiet moment.
>
> Give them a back rub after a long day.
>
> Initiate a spontaneous hug or kiss to show affection.

Personalizing Romantic Gestures

> ❝ *"Sometimes, the smallest things take up the most room in your heart"*
> — Winnie the Pooh

Personalized Romantic Gestures

Activity Templates

Shared activities are at the heart of creating memorable experiences with your partner. Whether it's a playful challenge, a creative project, or a simple adventure, these moments bring you closer together while adding a spark of excitement to your relationship. This section offers ready-to-use templates to help you plan and personalize unique activities for every occasion.

How to Use This Section

- Choose an activity that fits your current mood, schedule, and interests.
- Use the templates as a starting point and make adjustments to reflect your partner's personality or preferences.
- Focus on enjoying the process together rather than striving for perfection.

Activity 1: Scavenger Hunt for Two

How It Works:

Plan a scavenger hunt with clues leading to meaningful locations or surprises. Each stop can reflect a shared memory, an inside joke, or something your partner loves.

Template:

1. Start Point: Where will the scavenger hunt begin?
2. Clue #1: What's a riddle or hint that will lead your partner to the next location?
3. Stops Along the Way: Choose 3-5 meaningful places or items to include.
4. Final Surprise: End with a small gift, a heartfelt note, or a shared treat like dessert or wine.

Tip: Add personal touches, such as including a clue about the first place you met or your partner's favorite café.

Plan Your Activity

66 *"The best thing to hold onto in life is each other."*
— Audrey Hepburn

Activity 2: Dream-Date Vision Board

How It Works:

Create a visual collage together that represents your ideal dates and shared adventures. Use magazines, printed photos, or drawings to design a board that inspires future plans.

Template:

1. Gather Supplies: Collect scissors, glue, markers, magazines, or printouts.
2. Sections to Include:

   Dream destinations.

   Activities you want to try.

   Words or quotes that inspire you.
3. Add a Personal Flair: Include photos of past dates or inside jokes to make it uniquely yours.

Tip: Display the board somewhere you can both see it as a reminder to plan your next adventure.

Plan Your Activity

" *"Life is an adventure best lived together."*
— Unknown

Activity 3: Time Capsule for Two

How It Works:

Create a time capsule with notes, photos, or mementos from your relationship to open together in the future.

Template:

1. Gather Items: Choose 5-10 items that represent your relationship (e.g., concert tickets, photos, or letters).
2. Write Notes: Each partner writes a letter reflecting on the relationship and their hopes for the future.
3. Choose a Date: Decide when you'll open the capsule (e.g., a one-year or five-year anniversary).
4. Seal and Store: Find a safe place to keep the capsule until it's time to open it.

Tip: Include a playful promise, like trying something new together before opening the capsule.

Plan Your Activity

66 *"In every shared moment, we build the story of us."*
— Unknown

Part 2: Resources and Inspiration

Further Reading and Listening

In the ever-evolving journey of love and connection, knowledge and inspiration are invaluable. This section offers a curated list of books, podcasts, and online resources to complement the ideas in this handbook. Each recommendation is carefully chosen to deepen your understanding of relationships, enhance communication, and spark creativity in dating.

How to Use This Section

- Browse the categories and choose resources that resonate with your interests or current relationship needs.
- Use these materials as a starting point for learning and discussion with your partner.
- Revisit this list whenever you're seeking fresh insights or inspiration.

Category 1: Emotional Intelligence and Communication

Books:

- *Emotional Intelligence 2.0* by Travis Bradberry and Jean Greaves
- *Nonviolent Communication: A Language of Life* by Marshall B. Rosenberg
- *Dare to Lead* by Brené Brown

Podcasts:

- *Where Should We Begin?* with Esther Perel
- *Unlocking Us* with Brené Brown
- *The Happiness Lab* with Dr. Laurie Santos

Articles/Online Resources:

- "How to Improve Emotional Intelligence in Relationships" – Psychology Today
- "The Science of Listening: How to Truly Hear Your Partner" – Greater Good Magazine

Category 2: Mindfulness in Relationships

Books:

- *The Power of Now* by Eckhart Tolle
- *Radical Acceptance* by Tara Brach
- *Love for Imperfect Things* by Haemin Sunim

Podcasts:

- *Ten Percent Happier* with Dan Harris
- *On Being* with Krista Tippett
- *Meditative Story*

Articles/Online Resources:

- "Mindfulness for Better Relationships" – Mindful.org
- "The Role of Presence in Building Connection" – Harvard Health Publishing

Category 3: Creativity and Adventure in Dating

Books:

- *The Art of Gathering: How We Meet and Why It Matters* by Priya Parker
- *Big Magic: Creative Living Beyond Fear* by Elizabeth Gilbert
- *Wild at Heart* by John Eldredge

Podcasts:

- *The Adventure Zone*
- *Outdoor Explorer*
- *She Explores*

Articles/Online Resources:

- "How to Plan an Adventurous Date" – REI Blog
- "Creative Ideas for Couples" – Better Help

Category 4: Modern Dating Tools and Strategies

Books:

- *Modern Romance* by Aziz Ansari
- *The New Rules of Love, Sex, and Dating* by Andy Stanley
- *Attached: The New Science of Adult Attachment* by Amir Levine and Rachel Heller

Podcasts:

- *The Dating Podcast*
- *Love, Lust, and Boundaries*
- *Dating Kinda Sucks*

- "How to Use Dating Apps Effectively" – The Verge
- "Online Dating Tips from Behavioral Scientists" – Psychology Today

Category 5: Humor and Fun in Relationships

Books:

- *The Five Love Languages: The Secret to Love That Lasts* by Gary Chapman
- *Men Are from Mars, Women Are from Venus* by John Gray
- *Relationship Goals* by Michael Todd

Podcasts:

- *Funny in Love*
- *Love Is Funny*
- *Laughing Matters*

Articles/Online Resources:

- "The Role of Humor in Healthy Relationships" – Greater Good Magazine
- "15 Hilarious Date Ideas to Try" – Cosmopolitan

Category 6: Deeper Self-Understanding and Personal Growth

Books:

- *Man's Search for Meaning* by Viktor Frankl
- *Atomic Habits* by James Clear
- *You Are a Badass* by Jen Sincero

Podcasts:

- *The School of Greatness* with Lewis Howes
- *The Mindset Mentor* with Rob Dial
- *Optimal Living Daily*

Articles/Online Resources:

- "The Intersection of Personal Growth and Relationships" – Thrive Global
- "Becoming Your Best Self in Relationships" – Medium

Category 7: Resources for Niche Interests

For Long-Distance Couples:

- *Long Distance Relationships: Online Communication for Love, Intimacy, and Commitment* by Crystal Jiang
- "Creative Virtual Date Ideas" – The Spruce

For Adventure Lovers:

- *The Bucket List: 1000 Adventures Big & Small* by Kath Stathers
- "Planning Adventure Dates" – National Geographic Adventure

For Quiet and Reflective Types:

- *Quiet: The Power of Introverts in a World That Can't Stop Talking* by Susan Cain
- "Slow Dating: What It Is and Why It Works" – HuffPost

For Foodies:

- *Date Night In: More than 120 Recipes to Nourish Your Relationship* by Ashley Rodriguez
- "Cooking Together: The Recipe for Relationship Success" – Bon Appétit

Your Favorites and Takeaway

66 *"A good relationship is about learning, growing, and never stopping the adventure."*
— Unknown

Your Favorites and Takeaway

Glossary of Terms

In the world of dating, relationships, and emotional connection, certain terms and concepts can serve as guideposts, helping us navigate the complexities of love and partnership. This glossary offers clear, concise definitions of key terms used throughout this handbook and beyond. Whether you're diving into the language of intentional dating or exploring concepts of emotional intelligence, this section is designed to provide clarity and confidence as you deepen your understanding of relationships.

Organized alphabetically, this glossary ensures you can quickly find the meaning of any term. It's not just a reference but also a tool to spark reflection and inspire thoughtful conversations with your partner.

- **Acknowledgment**: Recognizing and appreciating your partner's efforts, feelings, or accomplishments.
- **Active Listening**: Fully concentrating, understanding, and responding thoughtfully during a conversation.
- **Affection Cues**: Subtle signs, like a smile or a touch, that signal love and care..
- **Affirmations**: Positive statements used to encourage and uplift your partner.
- **Attachment Behaviors**: Actions that demonstrate reliance and emotional bonding in a relationship.
- **Attachment Styles**: Patterns of behavior in relationships based on early life experiences; includes secure, anxious, avoidant, and disorganized styles.

- **Authenticity**: Being genuine and true to yourself in interactions and relationships.
- **Boundaries**: Limits you set to protect your emotional, physical, and mental well-being in a relationship.
- **Boundary Setting**: The act of establishing personal limits to protect emotional and mental well-being.
- **Burnout**: Emotional, physical, and mental exhaustion, which can impact the quality of a relationship.
- **Chemistry**: The natural connection and attraction felt between two people, often described as a "spark."
- **Collaborative Decision-Making**: A process where both partners contribute to choices that affect the relationship.
- **Commitment**: The decision to prioritize and invest in a relationship over time.
- **Compassionate Curiosity**: Asking questions with genuine interest and empathy during conversations.
- **Conflict Resolution**: Techniques for resolving disagreements constructively while maintaining respect.
- **Conflict Triggers**: Specific actions or words that cause disagreements or tension.
- **Conversation Starters**: Questions or topics used to spark dialogue and connection.
- **Daily Gratitudes**: A practice of sharing one thing you're grateful for in your relationship each day.
- **Date Debrief**: Reflecting on a date together to discuss what you enjoyed and learned about each other.
- **Date Night**: A planned outing or activity intended to strengthen intimacy and connection between partners.
- **Deep Dive Conversations**: Discussions that go beyond surface-level topics, focusing on values, dreams, and emotions.
- **Disarming Humor**: Using lighthearted jokes to defuse tension during conflicts.
- **Dopamine**: A neurotransmitter associated with pleasure and reward, often released during enjoyable shared activities.
- **Emotional Agility**: The ability to navigate your emotions effectively, particularly in challenging situations.

- **Emotional Availability**: The capacity to be open and responsive to your partner's emotional needs.
- **Emotional Deposits**: Positive actions or words that build trust and affection in a relationship.
- **Emotional Safety**: The feeling of being secure enough to express yourself without fear of rejection.
- **Emotional Validation**: Acknowledging and affirming your partner's feelings and experiences.
- **Empathy**: The ability to understand and share the feelings of another person.
- **Energy Alignment**: Matching your partner's energy levels to create harmony during shared moments.
- **Focus Time**: Intentional periods where you give undivided attention to your partner.
- **Forging Connection**: Actively seeking ways to deepen intimacy and understanding.
- **Forging New Traditions**: Creating unique rituals that define your relationship's identity.
- **Forgiveness**: Letting go of resentment and offering grace to a partner after a conflict or mistake.
- **Fun Dates**: Activities centered on laughter and play, designed to strengthen bonds through lighthearted experiences.
- **Generosity of Spirit**: Extending kindness, understanding, and patience in your relationship.
- **Gratitude**: The practice of recognizing and appreciating the positive aspects of a relationship.
- **Growth Mindset**: The belief that challenges and mistakes are opportunities for learning and development.
- **Habits of Connection**: Regular practices that foster intimacy and closeness in a relationship.
- **Healthy Conflict**: Disagreements that are managed respectfully and lead to mutual understanding.
- **Healthy Dependency**: Relying on your partner in a balanced way that fosters trust and support.
- **Healthy Space**: Taking time apart to nurture individuality without compromising connection.
- **Heartfelt Apology**: A sincere acknowledgment of a mistake, including an expression of regret and a plan to improve.

- **Inner Child Connection**: Acknowledging and nurturing the playful and emotional aspects of yourself in the relationship.
- **Intentional Dating**: Purposefully approaching dates with clear goals and a focus on creating meaningful connections.
- **Intentional Rituals**: Regular practices designed to strengthen bonds, such as a weekly date or nightly check-in.
- **Interdependence**: A relationship dynamic where both partners support each other while maintaining individuality.
- **Intimacy**: The close emotional and physical bond between partners, built through trust and vulnerability.
- **Joint Goals**: Shared objectives that partners work toward together, such as financial milestones or personal growth.
- **Joyful Rituals**: Small, repeated actions that bring happiness and consistency to a relationship.
- **Kindness**: The practice of showing compassion, generosity, and consideration in a relationship.
- **Listening With Intent**: Fully focusing on and understanding your partner's words without preparing a response.
- **Love Languages**: Ways people express and experience love; includes words of affirmation, acts of service, receiving gifts, quality time, and physical touch.
- **Love Maps**: Detailed knowledge about your partner's preferences, dreams, and values.
- **Loyalty**: Commitment and faithfulness to your partner and the relationship.
- **Maintenance Habits**: Small actions that consistently nurture the relationship, like daily check-ins or sharing a meal.
- **Micro-Moments of Connection**: Small, everyday interactions that build intimacy, like a smile or touch.
- **Mindful Dating**: Being present and intentional in the dating process, focusing on quality over quantity.
- **Mindful Touch**: Using physical affection to communicate care and presence intentionally.
- **Mutual Accountability**: Taking shared responsibility for the health and success of the relationship.
- **Mutual Respect**: Valuing each other's feelings, boundaries, and individuality within the relationship.

- **Nonjudgmental Communication**: Expressing thoughts and feelings openly without criticism or blame.
- **Nonverbal Communication**: Conveying emotions and intentions through body language, facial expressions, and gestures.
- **Novelty**: Incorporating new and exciting experiences into a relationship to keep it dynamic and engaging.
- **Open Communication**: Sharing thoughts, feelings, and concerns honestly and respectfully.
- **Oxytocin**: Known as the "bonding hormone," it promotes trust and emotional connection.
- **Personal Growth**: Individual development that enhances the quality of a relationship.
- **Playfulness**: Bringing humor and lightheartedness into the relationship to foster joy.
- **Playful Teasing**: Gentle humor that strengthens bonds without causing hurt or discomfort.
- **Quality Time**: Focused, undistracted time spent together to strengthen the bond.
- **Relationship Check-In**: A dedicated time to discuss the state of the relationship and address any concerns or goals.
- **Repair Attempts**: Efforts to mend a conflict or disagreement, such as humor or a kind gesture.
- **Responsive Touch**: Physical gestures that convey support, such as holding a hand during a tough moment.
- **Rituals of Connection**: Routine actions, such as goodnight kisses or morning greetings, that reinforce intimacy.
- **Romantic Gestures**: Thoughtful actions that express love and appreciation.
- **Shared Humor**: The unique jokes or sense of fun that strengthens a couple's bond.
- **Shared Vision**: A mutual understanding of values, goals, and dreams for the relationship.
- **Supportive Listening**: Providing encouragement and understanding during a partner's vulnerable moments.
- **Symbolic Gestures**: Actions or gifts that hold personal significance, like recreating your first date.

- **Time Investment**: Consistently dedicating quality moments to your partner and relationship.
- **Traditions**: Repeated activities or rituals that hold special meaning in the relationship.
- **Trust**: The confidence that your partner will act with integrity and care..
- **Understanding**: The ability to empathize with and validate your partner's feelings and experiences.
- **Vulnerability**: The willingness to be open and honest about your feelings, even when it feels risky.
- **Wonder Dates**: Activities designed to inspire awe and curiosity, such as stargazing or exploring nature.
- **X-Factor**: The unique qualities that make a relationship feel special and irreplaceable.
- **Yearning**: A deep desire for connection, often the catalyst for meaningful relationships.
- **Zen Moments**: Quiet, peaceful experiences shared with a partner that foster calm and presence

Part 3: Reflection and Journaling

Reflection Journal Templates

Relationships are the beautiful interplay of moments, memories, and emotions. Each shared laugh, quiet moment, and heartfelt conversation forms the threads of a bond that is uniquely yours. While the pace of daily life can often sweep us along, pausing to reflect allows us to truly appreciate and nurture our connections. Reflection isn't merely about revisiting the past; it's an opportunity to deepen understanding, foster gratitude, and create a foundation for growth. Through journaling, we bring these reflections to life, capturing not only where we've been but also where we hope to go.

The act of journaling transforms fleeting thoughts into tangible expressions of love, gratitude, and hope. Whether you're reflecting on a joyful date, processing a challenging moment, or envisioning the future, journaling provides clarity and insight. It gives you a space to explore your inner world while simultaneously strengthening your bond with your partner. Over time, these written reflections become a cherished record of your journey—a living testament to your shared story.

This section is more than a collection of writing prompts; it's a toolkit for growth, connection, and self-discovery. It offers a chance to celebrate the milestones you've achieved, express gratitude for the little things that make your relationship special, and set intentions for what lies ahead. By journaling, you make the intangible—feelings, dreams, and aspirations—real and actionable.

Why Reflection and Journaling Matter in Relationships

Reflecting on your relationship journey enhances your emotional intelligence, helping you recognize patterns, celebrate strengths, and address challenges. It fosters mindfulness, ensuring you remain present in your relationship while maintaining an eye toward its future. Journaling amplifies these benefits by giving your reflections structure and permanence. It encourages open communication, as shared journal entries can spark meaningful conversations, and it strengthens intimacy by creating a deeper understanding of each other's inner worlds.

What You'll Find in This Section

This section is designed to meet you wherever you are in your relationship journey, offering tools and prompts for every stage. Whether you're exploring a new relationship or looking to deepen a long-term bond, you'll find resources that are practical, accessible, and tailored to your unique connection. Key elements include:

- **Gratitude Prompts**: Exercises to appreciate the love, support, and joy your partner brings to your life.
- **Strengths and Growth Areas**: Reflections to celebrate what works well in your relationship and identify opportunities for improvement.
- **Milestone Journaling**: Spaces to capture and commemorate the big and small moments that define your journey together.
- **Relationship Check-In Templates**: Guided exercises to facilitate honest and constructive discussions about your partnership.
- **Dreaming and Goal-Setting Prompts**: Inspiring questions to envision your future together and align on shared aspirations.

How to Use This Section

Make this section your own. Use it individually for personal growth or together with your partner to deepen your connection. There's no right or wrong way to reflect—what matters is the intention you bring to the process. You might set aside a quiet evening for journaling, incorporate it into a date night, or use the prompts as conversation starters during a long walk. However you approach it, let this space be one of honesty, curiosity, and care.

The Value of Written Reflections

Writing down your thoughts solidifies them in a way that conversation alone cannot. It helps you process emotions, uncover insights, and create a tangible record of your growth. Revisiting past entries allows you to see how far you've come as individuals and as a couple. It's a reminder of the work you've put into your relationship and the love that sustains it.

As you begin this journey of reflection, know that each prompt, journal entry, and shared moment brings you closer to creating a love that is not only enduring but also deeply fulfilling. Let these pages be a space of creativity, connection, and celebration—a gift you give to yourself, your partner, and your relationship.

Reflection Prompts

Journaling is a deeply personal process, yet it can also be a shared adventure. These prompts are designed to spark introspection and meaningful conversations, whether you choose to answer them individually or with your partner. Each set of prompts focuses on a specific aspect of your relationship, helping you explore what makes your connection unique, celebrate your growth, and dream about what's next.

Take your time with these prompts. Some may resonate immediately, while others might require deeper thought. There's no rush—your journey through these questions is just as important as the answers themselves. Use this space as an opportunity to reflect honestly, to honor your shared story, and to foster a greater appreciation for the relationship you're building.

Gratitude Prompts

Gratitude is a cornerstone of a strong and joyful relationship. These prompts encourage you to recognize and celebrate the small, meaningful moments that make your partnership special.

- What's one thing my partner did recently that made me feel loved or appreciated?
- What are three qualities I admire most about my partner?
- When was the last time my partner surprised me in a wonderful way, and how did it make me feel?
- How has our relationship added joy or meaning to my life this past month?
- What's a shared memory that I feel especially grateful for, and why?

Strengths and Growth Areas

Understanding what works well in your relationship—and what could improve—empowers you to build a stronger connection. These prompts guide you in identifying those areas with clarity and compassion.

- What is one thing that we do exceptionally well as a couple?
- How do we support each other's goals and dreams?
- What's one area where we could communicate more effectively?
- How do we handle conflicts, and what could we do to improve?
- What's one habit or routine that strengthens our relationship?

Memorable Moments

The moments you cherish are the building blocks of your relationship. Reflecting on these experiences helps deepen your appreciation for the journey you've shared.

- What is a date we went on that still makes me smile, and why?
- What's a small, everyday moment with my partner that meant a lot to me?
- How do we celebrate milestones or special occasions, and what stands out as a favorite memory?
- What's one challenge we faced together, and how did we grow as a result?
- What's a place or activity that feels particularly meaningful to our relationship?

Dreaming and Goal-Setting Prompts

Looking ahead helps ensure that your relationship continues to grow and evolve. These prompts inspire conversations about your shared vision and the future you're building together.

- What's one thing I'd love for us to experience together in the next year?
- How can we better align our individual goals with our shared vision as a couple?
- What's a dream destination we'd like to visit together, and why?
- What are three new activities or hobbies we could explore as a couple?
- How can we create more time for each other in our daily lives?

Your Reflections

❝ *"Gratitude turns what we have into enough, and more."*
— *Melody Beattie*

Your Reflections

Relationship Check-In Template

Strong relationships thrive on open communication and mutual understanding. A regular relationship check-in is an opportunity to pause, reflect, and align with your partner. It's not about perfection but about staying connected, addressing challenges together, and celebrating your successes as a team. This template provides a guided framework to help you discuss what's working, what could improve, and what you both envision for the future.

Set aside uninterrupted time for this check-in—perhaps during a quiet evening or as part of a date night. Approach the conversation with curiosity, kindness, and a willingness to listen. Remember, the goal is to strengthen your bond, not to assign blame or dwell on mistakes.

Check-In Guide

1. Gratitude and Positivity

   What's one thing I've appreciated about you recently?

   What's a moment from the past week or month that made me feel especially close to you?

   How have we supported each other in ways that felt meaningful?

2. Strengths in Our Relationship

What's something we're doing well as a couple?

How have we grown or improved as a team over the past few months?

What's a habit or ritual that helps us stay connected?

3. Opportunities for Growth

What's one area where we could improve as a couple?

How can I better support your needs or goals?

Is there anything I've done that hurt or frustrated you, and how can I address it moving forward?

4. Shared Vision and Goals

What's something we're excited about or looking forward to in the near future?

What's one goal we'd like to work on together, and what steps can we take to achieve it?

How can we create more moments of joy and connection in our relationship?

5. Closing with Love and Appreciation

What's one thing I love about us?

How can we end this conversation on a positive and uplifting note?

Is there something we'd like to do now or soon to celebrate our relationship?

Tips for a Successful Check-In

- **Set the Scene**: Choose a relaxed, comfortable environment where you can talk without distractions.
- **Listen Actively**: Focus on your partner's words, validating their feelings and perspectives.
- **Stay Positive**: Frame the conversation as an opportunity for growth rather than criticism.
- **Follow Up**: Revisit any action items or goals you've discussed to ensure progress and accountability.

Our Relationship Check-In

Our Relationship Check-in

Celebrating Milestones

Every relationship is a collection of moments—some that pass quietly and others that leave an indelible mark on your shared story. Milestones are those standout moments that signify growth, triumph, or simply the joy of being together. They don't have to be grand or dramatic to matter; even the simplest milestones, like celebrating your first movie night or cooking a favorite dish together, hold meaning when approached with intention.

Why are milestones so important? Because they provide an opportunity to pause and reflect. In the hustle of daily life, it's easy to overlook the progress you've made as a couple. Milestones act as anchor points, allowing you to celebrate not just what you've achieved but also who you've become through the journey. By intentionally marking these moments, you strengthen your bond, deepen your appreciation for each other, and build a legacy of shared joy and resilience.

This section is about more than marking occasions—it's about weaving celebration into the fabric of your relationship. From reflecting on what a milestone represents to finding meaningful ways to commemorate it, you'll discover how these moments can enrich your partnership in lasting ways.

Guiding Questions for Celebrating Milestones

Reflection is at the heart of meaningful celebration. These questions will help you explore the significance of your milestones and create celebrations that honor your journey as a couple.

1. Reflect on the Moment

> What does this milestone mean to us as a couple?
>
> How have we changed or grown together since our last milestone?
>
> Is there a specific challenge we've overcome that makes this moment especially meaningful?
>
> What's a memory from this milestone that we want to carry forward?

2. Express Gratitude

> What am I most thankful for about our relationship at this stage?
>
> How has my partner supported or inspired me leading up to this milestone?
>
> What's one thing about our connection that I never want to take for granted?

3. Celebrate with Intention

> How can we honor this milestone in a way that feels authentic to us?
>
> Should we create a new tradition or ritual around this type of celebration?
>
> How can this celebration inspire or motivate us as we look toward the future?

4. Document the Milestone

> How can we preserve this moment—through words, photos, keepsakes, or a shared activity?
>
> What feelings or reflections do we want to record about this milestone?
>
> Is there a way to revisit this milestone in the future, like creating a time capsule or journal entry?

Examples of Milestones to Celebrate

Milestones come in many forms. Some are traditional, while others might be unique to your relationship. The key is to recognize and cherish them as markers of growth and joy.

- **Firsts**: First date, first trip, first big adventure together.
- **Anniversaries**: Yearly markers of your time together, but also fun ones like "our 100th inside joke" or "50th walk in the park."
- **Life Events**: Moving in together, starting a new chapter like a career or relocation, or welcoming a child.
- **Overcoming Challenges**: Successfully navigating a difficult time or reaching a shared goal.
- **Spontaneous Milestones**: That unexpected perfect day, an unforgettable laugh, or a moment that strengthened your bond.

Meaningful Ways to Celebrate Milestones

Celebration can take many forms, from quiet reflection to grand adventures. The most important thing is that it feels authentic to you and your partner. Here are some ideas to inspire your own traditions:

1. Recreate the Memory

    Revisit the place where the milestone happened or
    replicate the experience.

    For example, dine at the restaurant where you had
    your first date or recreate a favorite adventure.

2. Create Something Together

    Collaborate on a scrapbook, video, or time capsule to
    capture the essence of your milestone.

    Write letters to your future selves or create a vision
    board of what you hope to achieve as a couple.

3. Give a Thoughtful Gift

    Personalized tokens, like a photo book, engraved
    keepsake, or a playlist that represents your journey.

    Consider gifts that reflect inside jokes or shared
    interests for a personal touch.

4. Plan a Unique Celebration

    Take a day off for a "milestone adventure," like
    exploring a new city or trying an exciting activity.

    Host a private celebration, such as a picnic under the
    stars or a candlelit dinner at home.

5. Establish Traditions

    Create a ritual around specific milestones, like always
    writing each other a letter on anniversaries.

Celebrate "mini milestones," such as monthly date nights or quarterly reflections.

Tips for Making Milestones Meaningful

1. **Be Present**: Focus entirely on the moment and your partner. Turn off distractions and immerse yourself in the celebration.
2. **Collaborate**: Plan your celebrations together to ensure they resonate with both of you.
3. **Balance Big and Small**: Alternate between grander celebrations for major milestones and simple, heartfelt gestures for smaller ones.
4. **Make It Personal**: Incorporate elements unique to your relationship—shared hobbies, favorite places, or inside jokes.
5. **Capture the Moment**: Whether through journaling, photos, or souvenirs, find a way to preserve the memory for years to come.

Celebrating Our Milestones

"The magic of milestones isn't in the passing of time, but in the moments that take our breath away."
— Unknown

Celebrating Our Milestones

Celebrating Our Milestones

Conclusion to Reflection and Journaling

As we draw this section to a close, it's worth pausing to reflect on the purpose of reflection itself. Relationships thrive on communication, intentionality, and a shared understanding of growth and connection. Journaling isn't just a tool for capturing memories—it's a way to deepen your emotional bond, celebrate your shared journey, and align your dreams for the future.

Throughout this section, we've explored ways to cultivate gratitude, assess strengths and areas for growth, mark milestones, and dream together. These practices are designed to bring clarity and joy to your relationship, transforming abstract emotions into tangible actions. By engaging with these prompts and templates, you create a living record of your love story—a treasure trove of moments, lessons, and aspirations.

Remember, there's no "right way" to journal. Whether you write daily, weekly, or whenever inspiration strikes, the act of putting pen to paper is an act of care—for yourself, your partner, and your relationship. It's a space for honesty, vulnerability, and creativity, free from judgment or expectation.

As you continue on this journey, let your journal be a companion. Use it to revisit cherished memories, process challenges, and dream boldly about what lies ahead. Relationships are a beautiful balance of the everyday and the extraordinary, and this journal is your canvas to celebrate both.

Above all, remember that reflection isn't just about looking back—it's about moving forward with intention, gratitude, and love. By creating space for reflection and journaling, you invest in your relationship's future, ensuring that each chapter of your story is as meaningful as the last.

"Love After Love"

by

Derek Walcott

The time will come
when, with elation,
you will greet yourself arriving
at your own door, in your own mirror,
and each will smile at the other's welcome,

and say, sit here. Eat.
You will love again the stranger who was yourself.
Give wine. Give bread. Give back your heart
to itself, to the stranger who has loved you

all your life, whom you ignored
for another, who knows you by heart.
Take down the love letters from the bookshelf,

the photographs, the desperate notes,
peel your own image from the mirror.
Sit. Feast on your life.

"Variations on the Word Love"

by

Margaret Atwood

This is a word we use to plug
holes with. It's the right size for those warm
blanks in speech, for those red heart-
shaped vacancies on the page that look nothing
like real hearts. Add lace
and you can sell it.

We insert it also in the one empty
space on the printed form
that comes with no instructions. There are whole
magazines with not much in them
but the word love, you can
rub it all over your body and you
can cook with it too. How do we know
it isn't what goes on at the cool
debaucheries of slugs under damp
pieces of cardboard?

As for the weed-seedlings nosing their tough snouts up
among the lettuces, they shout it.
Love! Love! sing the soldiers, raising
their glittering knives in salute.

Then there's the two
of us. This word
is far too short for us, it has only
four letters, too sparse
to fill those deep bare

vacuums between the stars
that press on us with their deafness.

It's not love we don't wish
to fall into, but that fear.
this word is not enough but it will
have to do. It's a single
vowel in this metallic
silence, a mouth that says
O again and again in wonder
and pain, a breath, a finger-grip
on a cliffside. You can
hold on or let go.

www.ingramcontent.com/pod-product-compliance
Lightning Source LLC
Chambersburg PA
CBHW020420150626
46554CB00014B/2302